MR. WALKER:

THE CUSTODIAN AT OUR SCHOOL

DOSHIE WALKER, PhD

AuthorHouse™
1663 Liberty Drive
Bloomington, IN 47403
www.authorhouse.com
Phone: 1 (800) 839-8640

Published by AuthorHouse 06/14/2018

ISBN: 978-1-5462-3960-4 (sc)
ISBN: 978-1-5462-3961-1 (e)

Print information available on the last page.

author**HOUSE**®

CONTENTS

DEDICATION

This book is dedicated to my God and my family. With God, all things are possible. To my husband Karl, the love of my life, my companion, and my best friend. May you always find comfort in the man cave. To my daughter, who has grown into an intelligent and beautiful woman. You are my greatest source of pride. May you prosper and realize your fondest dreams. To my mother Ruth McNeal, and my mother-in-law Irenia Walker, who taught us the power of prayer, perseverance, and unconditional love. We know what love is and continue to share our love with our families and helping others.

ACKNOWLEDGMENTS

This is a loving collaboration with my spouse and daughter. The key idea of these stories is to show that no matter your profession, title or education, we all have a role to play in the world. Mr. Walker is the Head Custodian at a public school in Seminole County in Florida. These are his interactions where he has the privilege to make a difference in the lives of others daily. Be Blessed!

Smile

Mr. Walker is the Head Custodian at our school.
He always smiles and makes everyone happy to be at school.

Unhappy

On days when I feel sad, Mr. Walker says "think about the good things you are learning today" such as Music, Art, English, Math, Science and playing with your friends.

Sick

When I am sick, Mr. Walker tells me, you will feel better soon. Go to the nurse's office to see Mrs. Orange and she will take care of you.

Birthday Song

The students always remind Mr. Walker when it is their birthday, or the teachers tell Mr. Walker.

Mr. Walker announces during lunch all the students who are celebrating a birthday.

Mr. Walker starts singing the birthday song and everyone in the cafeteria join in and sing loud.

Mr. Walker gives everyone celebrating a birthday a pencil with the words "Happy Birthday."

Trivia Questions

Mr. Walker helps us learn different subjects by asking trivia questions. He asks us questions about math, American History, and American government, which helps me to remember some of the subjects I have learned.

When students get the question right, Mr. Walker gives us a high-five.

Mom's for Muffins and Dad's for Donuts

Mr. Walker is very busy most days setting up extraordinary events in the cafeteria.

On *Mom's for Muffins Day*, moms come to the school to eat muffins with their children.

Another special event day is *Dad's for Donuts*, when dads come to the school to eat breakfast with their children.

Mr. Walker makes our parents feel welcomed to the school.

Fundraisers

Mr. Walker helps with fundraisers at the school.

Mr. Walker sets up tables with food and games.

I love reading books and I can tell when the book fair is coming; Mr. Walker set up the tables and clean the area for the mobile book fair.

Physical Education

Sometimes Mr. Walker joins in the physical education classes to do exercises with us and to learn about healthy foods.

ABC's and Colors

Mr. Walker helps Pre-K and the kindergarten classes by saying the Alphabets and the different colors. I like when Mr. Walker helps the class with learning because we laugh and have fun.

Dominoes

Mr. Walker visits the classrooms sometimes to teach us to play Dominoes. It's fun because we are learning math as we count the numbers on the dominoes.

Book Report

Mr. Walker comes to our class to hear us read our book reports. The class talk about presidents, civil rights, owning a business and many other topics.

When the fifth graders have their market day, Mr. Walker come and buy something from each of the students.

Mr. Walker always tells us "well done" on our products.

Fairy Tale Ball

Mr. Walker sets up the Fairy Tale Ball in the cafeteria for the second graders. We dress up as our favorite prince or princess. We have so much fun! Mr. Walker tells everyone how beautiful and handsome they look.

Fire Drill

On fire drill days, Mr. Walker helps students learn what to do when they hear the fire alarm.

Pizza

Mr. Walker helps the third-grade class on Pizza Day!
Mr. Walker delivers a lot of pizzas to the class…and the pizza's smell delicious.

Supplies

The fifth graders sometime help Mr. Walker give out supplies to teachers and put extra supplies on the supply shelves.

Veterans Day

Mr. Walker helps the teachers set up for Veteran Day. Mr. Walker brings in both his and his spouse military uniforms to place in the display window. Mr. Walker talks to us about serving in the United States Army for 22 years.

The Stairs

Today Mr. Walker put yellow tape on the stair rails. Mr. Walker said that some students have a challenging time seeing distances, so he puts the tape on the rail to make sure all students are safe.

The End of the Day

At the end of each day, Mr. Walker stands out in front of the school with a big smile on his face and waves goodbye to all the kids. His final words each day is "See you tomorrow."

ABOUT THE COLLABORATORS

Mr. Walker is the Head Custodian at a public school in Florida. Mr. Walker is a United States Army retiree.

Doshie Walker is the Human Resources Generalist at a university in Florida. She also, is a United Stated Army retiree. Doshie has a Doctor of Philosophy in Industrial and Organizational Psychology from a University in Arizona.

Yazmin Walker is the daughter of Karl and Doshie Walker. She has a Doctorate in Occupational Therapy from a University in Florida.

Printed in the United States
By Bookmasters